WHITHER ANARCHISM?

by Kristian Williams

to the
POIN†

2018

To the Point, a Division of **AK PRESS**
Whither Anarchism?
© 2018, Kristian Williams
ISBN: 978-1-939202-27-7
E-ISBN: 978-1-939202-28-4
Published by AK Press in April 2018
akpress.org | akuk.com

CONTENTS

Introduction

In the three essays making up this pamphlet, I do my best to explain my current thinking about anarchism.

In the first, "My Anarchism," I try as simply as possible to say what anarchism means to me, to convey my idea of what it is and my own reasons for adhering to it as a political philosophy. The second, "Whither Anarchism?" draws from recent histories and considers how today's anarchists relate to (or rather, *fail* to relate to) the ideas that originally animated the movement. Logically speaking, it ought to be possible to see a direct connection between these two pieces. But the gap separating them is exactly the problem I'm trying to point to. For my own short statement of belief in the first in no way answers the more serious challenges of the second. What it might take to correct this situation, to provide the necessary theoretical support for anarchist positions, to bridge the gap between the idea and the movement, is the subject of the third essay, "Revolutions, Scientific and Otherwise." It briefly considers the cultural and structural prerequisites for the kind of reassessment I advocate, though it ultimately represents a challenge rather than a solution. At the very most, it may mark a point of departure.

I am not in these pages offering a theory of anarchism, or an anarchist theory of society. I do not, for example, *argue* for freedom and equality, but merely assume their value and explore some of their implications. Likewise, these essays say little about the causes or nature of coercion and inequality in our present society, and are almost silent on questions of strategy and tactics. In one pamphlet of a few thousand words, representing merely a single individual's views, I trust these omissions are forgivable. In a political movement, however, especially one directed at destroying the existing power structure

> Judging from its current condition, one finds it hard to believe that the anarchist movement could function as an effective means for *anything*, and certainly not for the total transformation of society and the creation of a more just world. It is not even clear that *movement* is the right word for something so aimless, amorphous, and prone to spontaneous collapse.

and reshaping our entire society, such inadequacies may prove fatal.

I do not know if the liberation of humanity depends on the success of the anarchist movement. On the whole, I hope that it does not. For that movement at present does not serve its cause well. It is insular, directionless, and often delusional, characterized internally by purity tests and faction fights, externally by ineffectual militancy and moral outrage. In both respects, one sometimes gets the feeling that the movement is driven less by a political agenda than by the collective dysfunction of its adherents. Judging from its current condition, one finds it hard to believe that the anarchist movement could function as an effective means for *anything*, and certainly not for the total transformation of society and the creation of a more just world. It is not even clear that *movement* is the right word for something so aimless, amorphous, and prone to spontaneous collapse.

However, it is my hope that, despite everything, anarchism may someday transcend its present limitations and once again come to represent the highest ideals and aspirations of humanity, and that anarchists may make a distinctive contribution to the struggle for freedom and equality, and to the new world that the struggle seeks to create.

My Anarchism

I.

I am going to attempt a rather unusual thing. I am going to try to explain why I am an anarchist—not in the autobiographical sense, telling the story of how I became an anarchist, nor in the historical sense, relating my beliefs to those of the philosophical traditions and political movements composing anarchism. Those are the standard narratives by which we justify our beliefs, either the Haymarket Affair and the Spanish Civil War or "I was a teen-age punk rocker." Our reliance on such stories, deeply personal or historically remote, is I think related to both the theoretical and the political weaknesses of the anarchist movement. These stories may encourage an audience to identify with anarchism, either from nostalgia for its heroic period of struggle, or in sympathy with the experience of alienation, but they do not as a rule speak to either the content or the basis of our ideas.

What I want to offer instead is an attempt to outline my thoughts about what anarchism is, and my reasons for adhering to it—as simply as I can, in plain language, without reference to the major theorists, and without attempting to authoritatively define or demarcate the boundaries of the ideology.

II.

I believe the core of anarchism to be captured in the proposition that decisions must be made by those most affected by them. That is, in effect, the standard of autonomy, meaning self-guidance or self-rule.

That belief, in turn, relies on a pair of values, those of freedom and equality.

Of course, *equality* does not mean that all people are the same, or even that they are necessarily entitled to exactly the same things. Rather, it means that we are all *equally human*, and equally entitled to the respect and consideration worthy of a human being. That is, no individual's worth is inherently greater than that of any other, and therefore in similar circumstances different people should be able to expect like treatment, at least as far as the major institutions of society are concerned. Any difference in treatment requires some justification based on morally relevant considerations, such as differences in need, skill, commitment, experience, etc.

Equality further suggests that, as all humans hold the same basic dignity, there is some fundamental minimum of respect to which everyone is entitled. This introduces the idea of *rights*—the notion that there are limits to how human beings may be treated, and that those limits are universal. It follows that there is some standard below which no one should be allowed to sink. No one should suffer hunger, or homelessness, or medical neglect, for instance. And likewise, everyone should enjoy the opportunities and support needed to develop their intellect and their talents, to perform meaningful work, and to share in both the benefits and the responsibilities incumbent upon their community.

Congruently, by *freedom* I mean simply that people can live their lives without interference, arranging their affairs according to their own best judgment—and, what is more, that they enjoy practical opportunities to widen the scope of their possible activities. Freedom suggests of course that no one should be actually oppressed, that unnecessary restrictions on individual choice be removed, and encumbrances to the development of our full potential be lifted—but it does not suggest action without limits. A value of freedom is in fact its own limit, since freedom cannot, without contradiction, include the freedom to impose one's will on others, to bully and tyrannize, to exploit them, or otherwise to undermine another person's ability to experience and develop their own freedom in their own way.

III.

From these two values—freedom and equality—it is possible to

MY ANARCHISM | 5

derive the precept of autonomy I spelled out already. And, since human beings need to be able to cooperate in order to survive, this standard must be understood to apply at the collective as well as the individual level. On the one hand, my own freedom of action is necessarily limited by the rights, needs, activities, and perhaps even the very existence of other people. On the other, the establishment of society practically enlarges the range of one's possible actions over a much wider territory. We can achieve so much more together than any one of us could alone; in fact, outside of prison or similar circumstances, *each* of us enjoys a greater range of possible activity, owing to our social existence, than *any* of us could in isolation. Even the most solitary of amusements—reading a book in the bath, for instance—ultimately depends on the thought and labor of innumerable other human beings, spread across time and geography, ordered and coordinated within several types of organization. Simply getting the water from its source to your faucet—*hot*, no less—is a remarkable achievement both technically and socially.

Our society manages these tasks of coordination partly through hierarchies of authority and partly through exchanges in markets. Though there is sometimes debate as to which arrangement is best for a particular kind of job, the two forms coexist as mutually reinforcing mechanisms, and the result is that power and resources come to be consolidated into relatively few hands. The accumulation of resources brings with it a large measure of power, and to the degree that this power is accepted as legitimate, authority as well. Likewise, the accumulation of power grants one the ability to acquire and control additional resources. Sometimes this power is used to directly coerce individual people, but more routinely its application is impersonal, establishing policies and making choices which shape the conditions under which we all must live. From the layout of our cities, to the quality of our air, the language we speak, the length of the workweek, the college curriculum, the size of our families, the holidays we celebrate, the music in the airport—all of these are determined, directly or indirectly, by one or another kind of politics. They all find a place within overlapping systems of power. And so, too, do you and I.

In the tiered command structure, a relatively small number of individuals are entitled to make decisions affecting the lives of many, many others—and the more authoritarian the system, the less responsive those in power have to be to the needs, desires, preferences, and demands of the people they rule over. However, even those at the very top often feel their decisions to be dictated by the internal logic of the system itself. Market forces, bureaucratic inertia, political realism, and above all, the need to maintain their own position in the hierarchy all constrain their choices, such that even CEOs, senators, and generals cease almost to function as distinct individuals and find themselves increasingly defined by their roles, driven by the needs of their organizations far more than their own desires or values. Such arrangements are contrary to our ideas of freedom and equality, and represent the precise opposite of our notion of autonomy.

IV.

Of course, if society is to survive there must be some means of organization, but our organizations need not be hierarchical and need not be driven by the profit motive. Decision making might be deferred to the lowest practicable level, it could be made participatory and democratic, and it could unfold through deliberation and negotiation toward something approaching consensus. Importantly, this model could be applied to all the institutions in our lives—public administration, industry, neighborhoods, churches. To distribute power in this way, the wealth of society would need to be held in common, to be managed and apportioned by these same means.

The new society that results would be organized as a decentralized network of democratically-run institutions and voluntary associations. Neighborhoods would be controlled by the people who live in them, workplaces by the people who work in them, schools by the people who teach and learn there. These various groupings would be free to act independently, or to affiliate and coordinate their activities, according to which approach best suits their purposes.

But note that none of the terms I am proposing need be absolute. There is no point in insisting on *total* decentralization, *perfect* equality, *unlimited* freedom, and so on. There may yet be some sorts of activities most effectively or efficiently pursued by creating a single central clearinghouse, or adopting a level of standardization, or appointing a steering committee. Leadership, supervision, and even coercive authority may sometimes still be necessary. The important thing is that any such position, or the exercise of such power, would need to be understood as requiring at every stage a kind of justification. Minus such justification, accepted by the people affected, there must be clear mechanisms for eliminating these positions or lifting whatever restrictions have been imposed. The norm, the default, would be the equal, the participatory, and the free.

The democratization of both power and resources would spell an end to capitalism and class society, with its pyramid of owners, bosses, and workers. So too would it mean an end to the state, with its legislators, bureaucrats, and police. And what may be more challenging still, it would also demand of us all that we eliminate any stratification based on race, gender, ethnicity, nationality, ancestry, sexual orientation, age, physical ability, or any other prejudicial or extraneous consideration. That effort will require a careful examination of the ways power relations are encoded into our institutions, our cultural practices, our personal relationships, and even our subjective attitudes and the structures of our thought. These informal hierarchies are pervasive and often indistinct; they may confine us in ways we do not recognize or impel us in directions we neither choose nor understand. They make up, to a surprising degree, the texture and atmosphere of everyday life. And more so even than our laws, which can be repealed, and our governments, which can be abolished, and our rulers, who can be overthrown, our habits of deference and entitlement may rule us more subtly and thus more firmly, and may prove the greater obstacle to our own liberation. Equality, in other words, must be alive in our minds as a positive ideal. It is not merely the

Equality, in other words, must be alive in our minds as a positive ideal. It is not merely the *absence* of inequality or subordination. It requires a new sociability, perhaps a new subjectivity, formed both within and between us as we work together to re-order society and discover new ways of relating—as we, in short, learn both to exercise and to respect freedom.

absence of inequality or subordination. It requires a new sociability, perhaps a new subjectivity, formed both within and between us as we work together to re-order society and discover new ways of relating—as we, in short, learn both to exercise and to respect freedom.

V.

What it would be like to actually live in such a society it is impossible to know and difficult even to imagine. Anarchy would likely be as different from anything we have experienced as capitalism was from feudalism. The future is as remote as the past, and uncharted. Any attempt to imagine it in detail would surely be a task better suited to a novel than a short pamphlet, and preferably not an overly utopian novel (or an overly dystopian one). And yet the promise of a better life is precisely the reason for pursuing radical social change. I will venture, then, a couple general remarks.

We should start by admitting that, in strictly materialistic terms, for many of us, especially for relatively privileged groups in the first world, what is called the standard of living may see a decline. I hope and expect that under conditions of worker power and local control the sweatshops and strip-mines that presently make possible our steady supply of cheap consumer goods would vanish. We would, as a result, probably own many fewer things. On the other hand, those things that we do own, being made by people invested in their work and being produced with an eye to the pleasure of use rather than maximizing profits, would also likely be of higher quality—more carefully made, more durable, and more comely. (Imagine a pair of good boots made by a cobbler, measured to your feet, and a few outfits, tailor-made to fit your body, rather than racks of cheap sneakers and closets full of ill-fitting, badly-made garments, mass-produced by near-slaves half a world away.) Likely, too, we would look less to exchange economies to meet our needs and become more self-reliant, both at an individual and a community level. Gardening, both on personal and collective plots, may take on greater significance. And we may see a resurgence of traditional handicrafts such as quilting and woodworking, as well as the emergence of new practical arts.

In any case, I think it near to certain that the pace of life will slow, that we will spend less energy rushing from work to store to home and back, and worrying about deadlines, punch-clocks, subway schedules, and microwave dinners suitable for half-hour lunches. Our time will largely be our own, our days largely filled with the activities we choose for ourselves. No one need arrange his life in service of his job, when we could arrange our jobs to fit well with our lives. Tedious, uninteresting, disagreeable work will not of course vanish, but there will be much less of it and, given the freedom to do so, workers may find ways to make it much less tiresome and unpleasant.

We would, moreover, be relieved of the burden of worrying always about money. The fear of the boss and the landlord—ultimately, the fear of unemployment and homelessness—are nearly universal in our present society and make up the background for almost every decision. In a society organized such that everyone had their basic needs met, in which no one was left destitute, such factors simply would not exist. Not only would this free us from the small tyrannies that presently control much of our day-to-day lives, it would also remove that constant sense of low-level dread (and, occasional, high-level terror), the persistent fear of losing our footing on whatever meager perch we have obtained and plummeting into the gutter—homeless, hungry, cold, abandoned, with no resources and no prospects. Free of such fear, even the narrow economic side of life must take on a different air. Our choices about work, about housing—really, about what we do and where we live—might be at last freely chosen, rather than pressed upon us, or grasped out of desperation.

So, too, our social relations must be very different. No one's role would be determined, or assumed, based on their race, gender, sexuality, nationality, or what their parents did for work. Diversity of all kinds should flourish, but differences of status would practically disappear. To be able to look one another in the face and address one another entirely as equals, even across difference, without barriers of inequality, would change the entire context and perhaps even tone of our quotidian interactions. Women, queers, people of color, and other historically marginalized groups would at last participate in society as full members. Such inclusiveness would, I strongly believe, benefit everyone, even those white men who had previously enjoyed privileged positions in the hierarchy. For as social barriers fall, as the stigma of inequality fades, our ability to relate to one another improves, becomes more natural, less fraught. We all profit from the contact with a wider array of perspectives, experiences, insights.

As society becomes more diverse, both within and among communities, and as it becomes more equal, it will, for that very reason, foster a healthy individuation that in turn feeds its diversity. None of us are free when we are locked in a framework of inequality; one's very position restricts one's possibilities, narrows one's vision, dictates much of one's behavior. Under conditions of equality, we are more free to be, and to become, our fullest selves. Among equals, we become more free.

> The creation of this sort of society, or anything like it, would require a kind of revolution, and that is true no matter what means are used to bring it about. For revolution denotes the *extent* of social change, not the method for achieving it.

VI.

The creation of this sort of society, or anything like it, would require a kind of revolution, and that is true no matter what means are used to bring it about. For revolution denotes the *extent* of social change, not the method for achieving it. Likely the revolutionaries will employ a wide array of tactics, experiment with competing and even contradictory strategies, and aim at different outcomes in different places. Progress will come erratically, unevenly, and not according to anyone's timetable. Likely it will not even look like a revolution as it unfolds, but as a series of crises, small miracles, wrenching compromises, painful defeats, stupid missteps, heroic sacrifices, frustrating reversals, bold experiments, regrettable excesses, ridiculous half-measures, reckless gambles, and righteous refusals—until finally, slowly, the overall shape of the new society begins to emerge, and the direction of events becomes clear. None of this is inevitable, however, and there is no guarantee that the outcome will be what we want.

Our successes are likely to prove both inspiring and disappointing. The reality will never exhaust the ideal: Our best attempts may approach it, but will inevitably fall short. Yet even our failures offer us lessons, if only we will learn them. Our successes, too, demonstrate the possibility of improving human life, but will also reveal to us new challenges—areas unexplored, injustices newly discovered and thus unaddressed. No success is ever total, no failure ever final. What we discover, in the interchange between them, is the idea of progress.

Even in the best society, life will often be hard. No doubt it will still contain a great deal of suffering, much of it pointless or even unjust. But in an anarchist society, for the first time, human beings will face each other as equals and the mass of humanity will collectively control the power by which we can create our own future.

The use of that power will bring with it new dangers, including the temptation to create new tyrannies, especially those based in moral purism, orthodox thinking, and social conformity. Therefore, even as we establish and employ our collective power, we must yet remain deeply skeptical about its justification and its claims. The use of power, even popular power, always calls for a great deal of wisdom, and care, and above all a growing sense of individual and collective responsibility—including a responsibility to and for each other. What we do then will be at last, and only, up to us.

VII.

The idea of anarchy is, I think, relatively simple, though I trust it is not simple-minded. Yet you have likely noticed how many more questions it poses than answers. Chief among these are those related to *how* the new society is to be brought about and, once it arrives, how it can defend and sustain itself. How are disputes to be settled,

The idea of anarchy is, I think, relatively simple, though I trust it is not simple-minded. Yet you have likely noticed how many more questions it poses than answers. Chief among these are those related to *how* the new society is to be brought about and, once it arrives, how it can defend and sustain itself.

especially challenges to the nature or structure of the society itself? How do we prevent new tyrannies from arising, especially tyrannies established in the name of *liberté, égalité,* and *fraternité*? It is all well and good to say that authority must be able to provide a justification—but what sort of justification? who determines whether it has done so, and how? and if it fails, what means would be available to dismiss it? Contrariwise, how do we interpret and elaborate the ideas of freedom and equality? How can they be built into the mechanisms of our institutions and the fabric of our culture? And can they be justified as limits to the actions of those who fail to see their value?

These are not easy questions, and it cannot be adequate to say that they will someday be worked out in practice, by others more free and enlightened than ourselves. For our answers to these questions, however tentative, must inform our actions in the present; they will shape our movements and guide our efforts. To translate our ideals into reality requires a strategy. It will not be enough to rely on our ethical sense and our desire for freedom. Any attempt to articulate a vision of the future will lead us quickly into questions, not only of politics and economics, but of sociology, anthropology, even psychology. We need to understand societies, cultures, people—how they function and how they change, what they are and what they might be.

Whither Anarchism?

No matter how one feels about it, the current state of anarchism represents something of a mystery: What was once a mass movement based mainly in working-class immigrant communities is now an archipelago of subcultural scenes inhabited largely by disaffected young people from the declining middle class.

Two recent studies have examined that transition from different angles. Andrew Cornell's *Unruly Equality: U.S. Anarchism in the Twentieth Century* carefully traces the political movement's trajectory from, roughly, the end of World War I to the end of the 1960s. It uncovers an organizational continuity between the earlier and more recent stages of the movement. Working, in a sense, in the opposite direction, Spencer Sunshine's dissertation, "Post-1960 U.S. Anarchism and Social Theory," begins by identifying the major theoretical currents of anarchism in the early twenty-first century, and tracks them back to their intellectual origins. He reveals a sharp *discontinuity* between post-sixties anarchist thinking and the social and political theories of the late-nineteenth and early-twentieth century Classical period. Crudely put, he finds that Zerzan, Bookchin, Graeber, and a number of lesser figures have little identifiable connection to Proudhon, Kropotkin, and Bakunin, and in fact draw their key concepts and arguments from entirely different philosophical traditions. The stories Cornell and Sunshine tell are in some sense complementary. Cornell tells of a political lineage obscured by a sharp ideological shift, whereas Sunshine detects a philosophical break hidden beneath the facade of a living political tradition. Crucially, both authors find contemporary anarchism in a state of confusion.

In what follows, I draw heavily from each of these histories to consider what anarchism has become, to recall how it has arrived in its present disordered state, and to propose a way forward.

PART ONE:
How We Got Here

Class War to Counterculture

In the early part of the last century, as recounted in *Unruly Equality*, American anarchism was predominantly, but by no means exclusively, syndicalist. It saw itself as a movement of the working class, fighting for the liberation of humanity from capitalism and the state, and it presented the labor union as the means by which workers could both overturn capitalism and organize the future society. The Industrial Workers of the World were of singular import. But the Red Scare of 1917–1920 all but destroyed the IWW, and with it the movement.

Anarchism came to comprise a set of cultural practices rather than a coherent movement or body of thought.

What remained of syndicalism was occupied primarily with legal defense, and other anarchists came to focus more on education and creating counterinstitutions, rather than mass organizing. Hence, anarchists were on the sidelines during the upheavals of the 1930s. Then, during the Second World War, the remaining movement split over the question of militarism, with pacifism becoming the dominant strain. At the same time, increasingly much of anarchist activity was in the cultural sphere, and the movement became wedded to the emerging counterculture. "[R]eadings, performances, and exclusive parties moved to the center of anarchist praxis," Cornell writes, "In the 1940s Bay Area scene, participating in such revelatory events became the primary activity expected of an anarchist. Indeed, we might interpret this as the time and place where an anarchist 'scene' emerged—exciting and socially rewarding to participants, but easily perceived as insular and exclusionary to those less connected."

Anarchism came to comprise a set of cultural practices rather than a coherent movement or body of thought.

On the positive side, the counterculture is what kept anarchism alive after it was decimated by the Red Scare. However, class struggle largely disappeared from the agenda and the movement became increasingly remote from its traditional base, producing a series of missed opportunities. Anarchists deserted the class war at precisely the moment that the largest number of workers were clamoring to enlist in it, leaving it to the Congress of Industrial Organizations and the Communist Party to benefit from the possibilities opened by the National Labor Relations Act. Nor did large numbers of anarchists agitate for a better New Deal, demanding additional benefits or opposing racial discrimination in the federal relief programs. Of course, given their theories and commitments—the view of the state as merely an instrument of the ruling class, the suspicion of legislative and bureaucratic reform, and the singe-minded emphasis on workplace organizing—it is not clear that anarcho-syndicalists could have done much better. In the midst of the massive changes brought on by the Great Depression, anarchists failed to take account of the ways Keynesianism was reconstituting both the economy and the state. Their doctrine thus became antiquated, their analysis atrophied, and they failed to adapt themselves to the opportunities and challenges of the new situation.

The Prefigurative Fallacy

The turn to pacifism also locked the anarchist movement in a particular "prefigurative" orientation.

Prefiguration has always existed in three forms: 1- the notion that our revolutionary organizations would later provide the means of coordinating and managing society; 2- counterinstitutions like anarchist schools, bookstores, co-ops, and utopian communities intended to displace governmental, clerical, and commercial institutions; and 3- lifestyle practices like free love and vegetarianism, which modeled egalitarian relationships and new, liberated modes of being. These different interpretations of "prefiguration" have received different measures of emphasis at various points in time. The IWW stressed the first; the Catholic Worker and the Modern School movement, the second; and the counterculture, the third.

Cornell quotes Holley Cantine, editor of the journal *Retort*, writing in 1942: "Communities and various other kinds of organization must be formed, wherein the ideals of the revolution are approximated as nearly as possible in daily life. The new society must be lived out by its advocates; both as a way of influencing the masses by example, and in order to iron out weaknesses of theory by actual experiment."

As it happened, little genuine *experimentation* resulted—either in the artistic sense of playful improvisation, or in the scientific sense of testing hypotheses against evidence. Instead, we have tried to compensate for our underdeveloped politics with an overdeveloped moralism, and anarchists became preoccupied with the minutiae of individual choice rather than organizing collective action.

This attitude rested on a contradiction inherent to the prefigurative idea. Morally, prefiguration demands that we act according to the principles of the society we want to create; and as strategy, it promises that we can create that society by doing so. The problem is that we are in no sense immune to the demands of the society we inhabit. Power relations and the barriers they erect are very real: legally, socially, economically, and even psychologically, our lives are constrained. Freedom cannot simply be *chosen*, it must be *created*. Were we capable of behaving as we would in a society without capitalism and the state, then there would be *no need* to abolish either. Instead, it is only possible to act as free and equal beings under conditions of freedom and equality; we cannot create those conditions simply by pretending they exist. The effort, at least as a whole politic, is in fact counter-productive since it turns our attention away from the structural features of our society and toward the moral character of individuals within the movement.

Moreover, the society that our present "anarchist communities" would seem to prefigure is not on the whole a place where sensible people would want to live. Such scenes are as status-obsessed, gossip-ridden, and cliquish as any private school, as prying and sanctimonious as any country church, as prone to splits and purges as the most rigid Leninist sect. Their chief virtues are that they are too small and disorganized to actually succeed in being particularly

We have tried to compensate for our underdeveloped politics with an overdeveloped moralism, and anarchists became preoccupied with the minutiae of individual choice rather than organizing collective action.

oppressive. Of course that is only part of the picture, but it is the part that an emphasis on prefiguration tends to foster. Trying to simply will the new society into being by means of personal virtue and exemplary group processes, we become harsh with each other for the smallest missteps. Every moment, every action, every word, every thought takes on an outsized importance, and a philosophy of total liberation produces instead a kind of totalitarianism writ small.

Turn, Turn, Turn

In his first book, *Oppose and Propose: Lessons from Movement for a New Society*, Cornell documented a more recent iteration of the cyclical exchange between pacifism and anarchism.

Beginning in 1971 the radical pacifist Movement for a New Society was active in environmental, anti-nuclear, and anti-war campaigns, bringing an explicitly anti-racist, feminist, class-conscious perspective to this work while also building counter-institutions like food co-ops and collective housing and training other groups in nonviolent direct action and consensus-based decision-making. Gradually, though, the group's internal dynamics—its processes, structures, and culture—proved incapable of meeting the demands generated by the group's political commitments. Consensus, prefiguration, and network structures were not enough to address questions related to leadership, race and class divisions, coalition-building, and informal hierarchies. These challenges, compounded by a lack of either the structures or processes necessary to resolve theoretical and strategic differences, ultimately led MNS to dissolve in 1988, but its imprint on the anarchist movement proved much longer lasting.

MNS never considered itself an anarchist organization, though it borrowed freely from anarchist ideas, including the works of Kropotkin, Berkman, and Bookchin. More striking, however, is the enduring effect this relatively small group had on the generation of anarchists that followed. In Cornell's assessment, MNS was "a major innovator and force in promoting, among other tools and approaches: multi-issue political analysis, consensus process, collective living and political community in urban areas, modeling political commitments in everyday relationships and life choices, network structures, identity-based caucuses, cost sharing and sliding-scale prices, direct action, and the use of spokescouncils" as well as "calling other activists out on their 'shit.'" This "litany of practices," Cornell notes without exaggeration, "seemed to define anarchists politics in the late 1990s and [early] 2000s."

After a few decades of pacifist-anarchist cross-pollination—exemplified, but by no means limited to MNS—we are left with the structure and culture of the pacifist movement without its commitment to nonviolence. Even when insurrectionary anarchism has come back into fashion, anarchists have tended to adopt by default many of the conventions and norms of the pacifists—only enlivened with fiery hyperbole and occasional window-breaking. The tactics, goals, and ideology may be different, but the style of politics is immediately recognizable. There is an *ethos* common to all surviving brands of anarchism—pacifist, syndicalist, platformist, nihilist, individualist, feminist, and green. It consists of a prefigurative insistence on modeling in our lives and our communities the values and practices of the society we wish to create; a ritualized emphasis on "direct action" tactics selected more for their expressive, symbolic, or cathartic qualities than for their actual effect; a strong affinity for (if not quite identification with) a specific subculture or counterculture; and a tendency to view ourselves as outside of and apart from society as a whole. More than any social theory or political objective, this cluster of traits tends to characterize contemporary anarchism and we seem to adopt them reflexively, almost automatically, and in some cases, even despite our own vocal criticisms of these qualities.

Toward the end of *Unruly Equality*, Cornell offers this assessment of "the legacy of U.S. anarchism": "Anarchists excelled at developing broad critiques of the social order. They were often ahead of the curve in identifying social problems (the oppression of gays and lesbians, environmental threats, the alienation of the affluent) and linking these issues to modes of domination.... Yet significant limitations are also apparent. In the twentieth century, anarchists were either uninterested or unable to systematize their perspective, and they have not excelled at engaging ideological opponents in an effort to win the war of ideas."

In the end, he concludes, with a tone of disappointment: "I am not convinced that anarchism possesses all the tools necessary to achieve [its] far-reaching goals."

No *Logos*

Picking up, in a sense, where Cornell leaves off, Spencer Sunshine's dissertation, "Post-1960 U.S. Anarchism and Social Theory," examines the course of anarchist thought (and, where relevant, political action) over the past half-century. Anticipating Cornell's conclusion, Sunshine writes: "Anarchism has lost its theoretical grounding. It has become an irreducible grab bag of elements, not just from the already fragmented tradition of classical anarchism, [but] also from a variety of other intellectual traditions.... Anarchists adopted ideas from movements as wide-ranging as deep ecology, biocentrism, and bioregionalism; various feminist and identity politics discourses; phenomenology; Kantianism; populist socialism; animal liberation politics; anti-colonialism; post-structuralism; chaos and emergence theory; situationism; and various forms of marxism, including the Frankfurt School, Third World Marxism, white privilege theory, autonomism, council communism, and the autonome."

Anarchist theory has become detached from its foundations in Classical Anarchism and instead has increasingly relied on ideas borrowed from other traditions, re-oriented toward anti-state conclusions.

Cornell's history traces the process by which anarchism moved from one phase to another while stressing the "clear line of continuity" between its Classical and current periods. Sunshine focuses on the result of the ideological shift: anarchist theory has become detached from its foundations in Classical Anarchism and instead has increasingly relied on ideas borrowed from other traditions, re-oriented toward anti-state conclusions. Thus theorists like John Zerzan and David Graeber have forwarded new, distinctive (and mutually incompatible) "anarchist" politics without drawing from traditional anarchist conceptions. Meanwhile, the major thinker of this period *most* connected to Classical Anarchism, Murray Bookchin, was precisely the one who renounced anarchism toward the end of his life.

At the same time, as Sunshine recounts, late-twentieth century anarchist *politics* were moving in an increasingly ecumenical direction, operating within and across other movements—environmentalism, organized labor, animal rights, anti-war—and anarchists fostered cooperation with other radicals, and even liberals, where it was possible to find common ground. Action took precedence over ideology, for good and for ill. On the one hand, the Teamsters-and-Turtles coalitions of the anti-globalization movement provided exactly the right environment for this approach to thrive, and anarchists enjoyed a moment of relevance and influence far beyond what our meager numbers would have suggested. On the other hand, the pragmatic emphasis on *practices* made it possible to conclude that the *ideas* simply do not matter. In *Freedom is an Endless Meeting*, an illuminating study of participatory decision-making in left-wing movements, Francesca Polletta quotes an unidentified member of the Direct Action Network as saying, "as long as you're willing to act like an anarchist now, we don't care what your long-term vision is." (David Graeber was one of four DAN members participating in the interview from which this quote is drawn.) In fact, as Sunshine notes, Graeber takes this thinking a step further, to suggest that anarchism is *only* a set of purely formal practices, and that any attempt to define its substantive program is inherently "vanguardist."

Sunshine doesn't trace the story out this far, but one can discern two further (bad) developments in the years following the anti-globalization peak. First, the formalist anarchism-as-practice-not-theory approach seems to have reached its logical conclusion in the 2011 Occupy movement. There the focus on *how* activists do things completely eclipsed any consideration of *what* they were doing or *why*, layering a prefigurative idealism overtop a rough collection of symbolic (though functional) tent cities and even more symbolic confrontations with police, with no coherent strategy or even agreed-upon aims.

The second, somewhat countervailing result is the frustration and impatience of more sectarian anarchists with the tame, lowest-common-denominator politics of leftist coalition work. An emerging tendency has sought to define anarchism primarily in terms of its uncompromising militancy, divorcing it from popular movements and positioning it not only outside of and apart from, but actively (and sometimes mainly) *against* the organized left. Somewhat perversely, this insurrectionist-cum-nihilist trajectory has proceeded with the same eclectic approach to ideology, sometimes inviting in ideas from the political right. Where efforts have been made to reconnect with the Classical Anarchist tradition, it is almost exclusively through the figure of Max Stirner—always a marginal contributor to the anarchist canon, precisely because of his distance from the socialist movement.

Lifestyle Anarchism?

This is hardly the first time anarchism has suffered an identity crisis. Two decades ago, in 1995, Murray Bookchin vented his frustration with the direction the movement was taking, publishing a polemic titled *Social Anarchism or Lifestyle Anarchism: An Unbridgeable Chasm*. In that short book, he sought to reassert anarchism's character as a mass movement by counterposing it to a "lifestyle" pseudo-politics. In describing "lifestyle anarchism" he denounced a whole range of ideological opponents, sometimes conflating incompatible tendencies. He also attempted to define away the entire individualist tradition in anarchism, and presented himself as an old guard defending "The Left that Was" against hucksters peddling zines and raves and vegan potlucks as politics. Though the problems with Bookchin's arguments were immediately evident and much discussed in the anarchist press at the time, "lifestyle anarchism" survives as a label affixed (always by others) to a wide range of norms, attitudes, and practices associated with the scene.

However, not only were the cultural and prefigurative aspects of anarchism not new when Bookchin was writing, the complaints about them were not new, either. Cornell quotes Harry Kelly, as far back as 1908, worrying that anarchism was becoming "a movement for individual self-expression rather than collective revolution." Sunshine directly links Bookchin's social/lifestyle dichotomy to a debate in the 1907 Anarchist conference in Amsterdam, mischaracterized in short order as a split between "individualists versus syndicalists": In that dispute, "Essentially all anarchists who were not focused primarily on organizing the working class into unions became labeled as individualists, regardless of their actual views about class struggle, the role of the individual, etc." Bookchin simply re-labeled "individualism" as "lifestyle anarchism" and absorbed syndicalism into the broader category of "social anarchism," but otherwise preserved the structure of the argument.

Naturally Bookchin could not acknowledge this intellectual debt. Not only would it reveal his sophistry in reframing an already dishonest argument from an earlier faction fight, but the very fact that there *was* an earlier controversy would undercut his portrayal of the movement's Golden Age. Anarchism has always included "hard-bitten shop floor organizers" *and* "new age hippie flakes" (to borrow Betsy Raasch-Gilman's terminology, quoted in *Oppose and Propose*). And the two types have not always gotten along well together. Bookchin's stoking of this perennial conflict did nothing to clarify the particular problems of the moment, though it did at least add a new term of abuse to the sectarian lexicon.

The anarchist concern with cultural and ethical questions was long-standing and deeply ingrained, but what *had* changed over the course of the century was the role of class struggle and the dominant *character* of the cultural and prefigurative efforts. In the late nineteenth and early twentieth centuries, the cultural aspects of American anarchism consisted largely of things like community theater and folk singing groups; in the teens, anarchism became associated with the artistic avant-garde; and after World War II, the counterculture. Likewise, prefiguration came to refer less to the kinds of organizations anarchists were building, and more to their individual choices. As a result of this drift, Cornell observes, "In the postwar period ... anarchists' prefigurative lifestyles and communities were less and less embedded in broader working-class traditions and neighborhoods, and they were not paired with confrontational class struggle."

Cornell's account—contra Bookchin's—suggests that if anarchism is in a bad state, that is not because of what was *added* in the postwar period, but what was *left out*. The renewed emphasis on gender and racial equality were crucial correctives to syndicalism's implicit tendency toward class reductionism. Likewise, the emerging ecological perspective and the attention to the environmental and psychological effects of industrialization fueled a sense of revolutionary urgency and suggested an agenda far beyond social egalitarianism and worker self-management. Bookchin, the chief theorist of "social ecology," at least agreed with that much.

Furthermore, the serious attention given the *means* of change, distinctive of anarchism since Bakunin's quarrel with Marx in the First International, really became *more* important as the century wore on. Not to put too fine a point on it, but in a period marked by two World Wars and the permanent threat of nuclear annihilation, pacifism must have had an inherent, immediate, intuitive appeal. And prefiguration, even of the "be the change" bumper-sticker variety, does at least recognize the necessity for individual transformation, though it happens to exaggerate its social effects.

The problem is, as anarchists retreated—not capriciously, or from a sense of superiority, but in direct response to the repression of the IWW—the movement necessarily changed, and its self-conception changed as well. Anarchists stopped thinking of themselves as a social force potentially capable of organizing millions of people, destroying the existing power structure, and reconstituting society. The *language* of revolution remained, but the *idea* was largely lost. The anarchist vision shrank, from the One Big Union and the General Strike, to the affinity group and the poetry reading. At first simply adapting themselves to a political reality—to the experience of defeat, alienation, and marginality—anarchists started defining themselves by those same features. They became enamored with their outsider status, at the expense of their broad, popular aspirations.

Anarchists stopped thinking of themselves as a social force potentially capable of organizing millions of people, destroying the existing power structure, and reconstituting society. The *language* of revolution remained, but the *idea* was largely lost. The anarchist vision shrank, from the One Big Union and the General Strike, to the affinity group and the poetry reading.

PART TWO:
Where to Now?

Reinventing Anarchism, Again (and Again)

There is however a hopeful implication to this story.

Pacifism moved from the margin to the center of anarchism, owing largely to historical circumstances: because anarchists and pacifists were forced together into prisons and labor camps during the Second World War. But the two tendencies did not merge automatically. Instead, the anarchist philosophy was deliberately being reconsidered, revised, and to a large degree reinvented by specific identifiable people—Ammon Hennacy, Dwight McDonald, and other writers associated with the journals *Why?* and *Retort*. Cornell quotes the poet Kenneth Rexroth: "Our objective ... was to refound the radical movement ... to rethink all the basic principles ... to subject to searching criticism all the ideologies from Marx to Malatesta." That fact logically implies that anarchism could be reinvented again.

Current attempts to create broad, public, formal anarchist organizations are in one respect a hopeful sign. They represent efforts to raise anarchism up from the underground, to break it out of its subcultural confines, and to engage again with the public at large without the mediating filter of the black mask. However, though such projects have been gaining steam over the past few years, they are themselves outliers in an already fragmented and marginal subculture. Groups like the Black Rose Anarchist Federation and the May 1 Anarchist Alliance, with their articulated principles and explicit strategies, are hardly typical of anarchism as a whole. Furthermore, while new organizations may be needed, they are clearly not *all* that is needed. For they will inevitably have to answer *in practice* the exact questions that anarchism has been evading with its peculiarly patchwork approach to theory. Actual organizing may have the benefit of sorting the significant issues from the superfluities, but it will for the very same reasons reveal how lacking our answers generally are.

Some of the unanswered questions, about how we organize society and why we favor the forms and strategies that we do, are fundamental and therefore quite old. However, no "return" to Classical Anarchism, or later variants like anarcho-syndicalism or insurrectionism, is possible or even really desirable. Capitalism, the state, social stratification, and the left have all changed—and both our theories and our movements need to address themselves to those changes. Besides which, many of the elements characterizing postwar anarchism—feminism, environmentalism, and an emphasis on fighting white supremacy, especially—are positive developments and brought needed emphasis to issues that were too often treated as secondary. Moving forward, any anarchism worthy of the name will have to incorporate these as essential features of its vision.

What we need is not a return, but a critical reevaluation—one that is, at once, both a deconstruction and a renewal. I have only a vague idea of what that reassessment would look like, but I do have some thoughts about the tasks it should prioritize and along what lines it should develop.

Old Ideals

I think the place any new anarchist theory should start is with re-centering the old ideals of freedom and equality. It is striking how little that language is used on the radical left anymore. Its neglect, I suspect, is partly down to a desire to distance ourselves from liberalism, and partly from the (related) postmodern suspicion of universalist claims. However, while both terms—*freedom* and *equality*—are abused by hacks and exploited in propaganda, that is precisely because they remain inspiring ideals that speak to something deep and defining in the human spirit. Furthermore they are, or at least they ought to be, *affirmative* ideals—not merely rejections of something else. To give them positive content, we need to be able to specify what we mean by the words, and further still, how our politics will bring these ideals into reality.

A positive formulation, I believe, need not be overly prescriptive—in fact, I think it should be diverse, pluralistic, and innovative—but it should offer some vision of what a diverse, pluralistic, and innovative society might be like; or, returning to the original meaning of an "anarchism without adjectives," it might present a range of possible models established according to some identifiable and common principles.

Better Critiques

Whatever form it takes, the very attempt at reformulation would demand a fundamental shift in anarchism as it is presently conceived, as essentially a philosophy of refusal. Furthermore, as it stands, *what* we are refusing is surprisingly uncertain and contentious. Are we against power, coercion, hierarchy, the state, government, privilege, domination, sovereignty, civilization, society, "the extant"—or something else entirely? None of those formulations quite do the job: They would all seem to include some things we probably do *not* oppose, and leave out some things that we certainly *do* oppose. The negative formulation of anarchism, as being simply *against* one or all of the above boogeymen, is responsible for a lot of our present theoretical underdevelopment, and the well-intentioned but misguided efforts to always stretch our tent further and cover more and more of the left's ideological circus.

Likewise, for a group so fixated on countering power and the state, it is surprising how rarely today's anarchists have bothered to put forward a theory about either one. It is as though we determined that they are bad, then decided to give the matter no further thought, as one might take a sip of milk, discover it sour, and simply spit it out. The inability or unwillingness to develop a theory of the state (or more modestly, an analysis of states), one that can take account of both the differences between governments and also the changes within them, has repeatedly steered the anarchist movement into blind alleys. In the thirties, the anarchists failed to take advantage of the opportunities presented by the New Deal; in the 1940s, the movement split over the question of whether democracy should be defended against fascism; and under neoliberalism, many anarchists have seen the necessity of fighting to defend and preserve welfare programs but lack any theoretical justification for doing so.

This short essay is not the place for a thoroughgoing theory of the state. But I suspect that such a project would need to begin with the recognition that states comprise *networks* of institutions, and that these institutions have different, sometimes competing—and even conflicting—needs, functions, strategies, and agendas. I further suspect that, even according to anarchist principles, different parts of the state must be approached differently. I doubt that anyone, in real life, has precisely the same attitude toward the police department, the water bureau, the IRS, the EPA, state universities, and the public library; there are some parts of the government we wish to abolish, and some we might want to capture and democratize. Other conclusions, concerning the differences between liberal and totalitarian governments, or the need to defend specific programs under certain circumstances, likely follow. On the whole, our opposition to the state would probably need to become less total and more strategic—not so much a smashing as a dismantling, with specified pieces to be recycled or repurposed.

At the same time, and congruently, anarchism needs to develop a broader theory of power. It should interrogate and integrate its recent borrowings from feminism, critical race theory, queer theory, indigeneity, and so on, relating them all to both the new analysis of the state and a (similarly updated) critique of capitalism and class society, while also being careful to avoid the various pitfalls of essentialism, nationalism, class reductionism, and the facile treatment of "classism" as another brand of prejudice. The resulting theory must be able to function at two levels simultaneously, understanding how these various forms of oppression and systems of power operate distinctly, on their own terms and by their own logics, *and* recognizing how they fit together, how they reinforce and shape each other, how they together structure the society we inhabit. That would require attention not only to the intersections where power is applied most acutely, but also to the cleavages where systems of power can be pried apart, and the interstices where liberatory practices and egalitarian relations may develop.

Theoretical Coherence

These tasks, which I have only roughly set out, would demand that we draw connections between our various ideas as part of some larger coherent body of thought. In contrast, as Sunshine details, the standard (non)theoretical practice has been to selectively adopt conclusions from disparate traditions without engaging the arguments for them. Individual ideas have survived, but in isolation from any theoretical framework that might give them support; they are advanced as principles, without reference to the reasons behind them. As a result, these notions cease to be working theories and become points of doctrine accepted on something like faith.

Both Cornell and Sunshine argue this explicitly. Cornell writes in *Oppose and Propose*: "Too often, aspects of political practice (for instance, the use of consensus, communal living, rejecting leaders, or following the leadership of those 'directly affected') are asserted as articles of faith, or assumed to be transhistorical tenets that anarchists ... have always practiced and therefore always should. When we don't know the origins of such ideas and practices, we have a harder time evaluating how useful they were under previous circumstances and if they are the right tools for the job given conditions today."

Arguing along the same lines, Sunshine is more cutting in his judgment: When "anarchism jettisons its possession of a (or any) coherent onto-epistemology" it risks morphing into "a faith-based movement." The result is both intellectual stagnation and political rigidity: "all fundamental questions are proclaimed to be resolved at the outset, ... making it difficult (or impossible) to have internal debate regarding the nature of the political movement itself. Which is to say: self-reflection on *why* anyone should hold anarchist political ideas is no longer possible.… If people do not *recognize* the basis of their critique, it is impossible to have a discussion about it with them; ideas end up being either accepted or rejected, but never really debated or worked through. This is neither anarchist nor democratic; in fact [it] is a serious intellectual devolution."

As an alternative, Sunshine proposes that we learn to relate our ideas to each other and to a more-or-less stable theoretical core, probably derived from the Classical canon (Godwin, Proudhon, Kropotkin, Bakunin, and maybe Stirner). Various observations, insights, concepts, and analyses would still surely be taken on from other traditions—but they would need to be approached at the level of argumentation and fitted together with other ideas central to the anarchist project, not (as at present) adopted as axioms and thrown together willy-nilly in what is sometimes too optimistically termed a tool kit. Anarchism would continue—as it always has—to incorporate innovations and insights from other political traditions, from the sciences and social sciences, from the arts and humanities, and to change and adapt our understanding of the world in light of new arguments and new information. But we should do so with attention to the reasons for these additions, their implications, and the ways they cause us to affirm or revise our previous theories.

> The willingness to look beyond our borders and outside the anglophone world is in itself a hopeful sign, but it is not a short-cut past the need for critical thinking.

The same care must be taken even when anarchists adopt *anarchist* ideas that emerged in different contexts—the distant past, for example, or other countries. Just as we cannot simply revive syndicalism (or, for that matter, egoism) without attention to the changes of the last hundred or so years, we likewise cannot just take a theory, practice, or tendency that has developed elsewhere—Greek insurrectionism or Latin American *especifismo*, for example—and adopt it *in toto*, without considering both the theoretical and the social context in which it arose, and the specific features that may or may not be translatable to our own present circumstances. The willingness to look beyond our borders and outside the anglophone world is in itself a hopeful sign, but it is not a short-cut past the need for critical thinking.

Ethics and Politics

Finally, or in practice, most pressingly—we need to distinguish between ethics and politics, recognizing that we do inevitably need both.

Ethics is concerned with matters of individual character, questions of right and wrong, and standards of conduct. Politics, in contrast, is concerned, both theoretically and practically, with the organization of society, the distribution of power and resources—not only narrow questions of policy, but more broadly the mechanisms by which those questions arise, how they are framed, and how they are settled. Political theory extends, importantly, beyond the ultimate shape of the society we want, and covers also the efforts to bring it into being—the organizations, institutions, movements, and even individuals that build, fashion, and sustain the social world. Politics, in other words, is a matter of both the means employed and the ends pursued.

There is obviously a relationship between the ethical and the political, and *justice* is a concept common to both. In practice, at the very least, our ethics should guide and constrain our politics, and our politics should inform and shape our ethics. Each in a sense relies on the other. Politics without ethics becomes indistinguishable from power-worship and bullying, while ethics without politics tends toward either a kind of saintly quietism or a meddling purism. However, though related, the two fields are necessarily distinct. *Because* we need ethics as well as politics, politics as well as ethics, it is necessary that we not conflate them.

The relationship between these two spheres of value is complicated, and cannot be reduced to questions of individual versus collective action, or means and ends—but the larger mistake tends to generate confusion in these other areas as well. It becomes too easy to believe that a good society is just the product of good people, and therefore that our movement's political failings are down to the sins of some one or a few of its participants. Likewise if (as the slogan goes) "the means are the ends," then radical means, like the moral virtues, are their own reward: they need not produce any tangible effect in the world. The tendency then is to view the movement itself as both the agent and the object of change. Our collective attention turns increasingly inward—more intensely scrutinizing the lives and attitudes of other anarchists according to constantly shifting and ever more exacting standards.

Of course there is no question that ethics matter, that individual actions sometimes affect large numbers of people, or that only by justifiable means can we reliably serve the ends of justice. But surely we can chart a course somewhere between Leo Tolstoy and Niccolò Machiavelli. In fact, the anarchist love of freedom ought to warn us against our own more puritan inclinations. Our prefigurative practices should be guided by a strategic need to avoid establishing new tyrannies, not by a moral demand that we fully realize some pristine utopia. In fact, among the tyrannies we should avoid creating are those based in perfectionism and moral purity.

Coda

I do not know what the outcome of this kind of critical reassessment would be, or whether anyone in our present circles possesses the philosophical acumen and political will to make the attempt. I do believe that if the movement's current condition persists—if anarchism remains only a loose assortment of social scenes with distinctive and often obscure norms and practices, collectively darting from one ideological fashion to the next, always seeking the newest or most radical-sounding slogans (rather like a crow chasing

If anarchism remains only a loose assortment of social scenes with distinctive and often obscure norms and practices, collectively darting from one ideological fashion to the next, always seeking the newest or most radical-sounding slogans (rather like a crow chasing a bit of tinsel on a windy day)—the movement will deteriorate until it is only an historical curiosity.

a bit of tinsel on a windy day)—the movement will deteriorate until it is only an historical curiosity, comparable to the Diggers or the Anabaptists. Without substantive changes within anarchism, it will never produce another revolution, much less a new society. It may, for all that, prove to be a transformative force in the lives of individuals who come into contact with it. Just as often, though, it will lead to exhaustion, disillusionment, and cynicism.

History does not provide a remedy for our present malaise. It does, however, help us to understand how it has developed. It invites us to consider why we believe the things that we do, whether the anarchism we have is the one that we want, and how we expect to make a better world.

These are basic questions, but so hard to answer.

Conclusion:
Revolutions, Scientific and Otherwise

In the defining work of his career, *The Structure of Scientific Revolutions*, the philosopher Thomas Kuhn proposed a model of scientific progress, whereby for long periods a field of study will advance through the patient collection of evidence and the testing of hypotheses within a dominant theoretical framework, a "paradigm." Gradually, however, this process of "normal science" produces and accumulates abnormal results, "anomalies" and unanswerable questions, until the existing paradigm becomes untenable. Science then enters a period of crisis, which is only resolved when a new paradigm emerges, one that can take account of the evidence, incorporate the anomalies into a coherent system, and productively investigate the hitherto perplexing mysteries.

Anarchism is badly in need of just this sort of paradigm shift. We have accumulated more than our share of anomalies, inconsistencies, absurdities, and quandaries. Unfortunately, however, anarchists are not engaged in normal science, even by analogy. The work of that stage (as characterized by Ian Hacking in his commentary on Kuhn's book) consists of: "(1) determination of significant facts, (2) matching of facts with theory, and (3) articulation of theory" (i.e., "bringing out what is implicit in the theory, often by mathematical analysis"). Like ideologues of all types, anarchists are instead prone to testing the facts against the theory, and simply ignoring the evidence that does not fit. Our unanswerable questions then become unaskable. To even pose them may as well be heresy, and will surely be seen as disloyal. When our theories are no longer tested against reality, they cease to be testable at all; and soon, they cease to be theories.

Anarchism seems to have entered a phase that Kuhn did not describe, in which one paradigm has collapsed, but no new paradigm has replaced it. All that remains are propositions and platitudes lacking any unifying structure, common premises, shared vocabulary, or agreed-upon methodology.

In the first paragraph of *After Virtue*, Alasdair MacIntyre imagines the conceptual confusion following a society-wide purge of scientific knowledge, producing a new Dark Age; then, decades later, "enlightened people seek to revive science, although they have largely forgotten what it was.... all they possess are fragments: a knowledge of experiments detached from any knowledge of the theoretical context which gave them significance; parts of theories unrelated either to the other bits and pieces of theory which they possess or to experiment; instruments whose use has been forgotten; half-chapters from books, single pages from articles, not always fully legible because torn and charred. Nonetheless all these fragments are remembered in a set of practices which go under the revived names of physics, chemistry and biology."

The language of science—"expressions such as 'neutrino,' 'mass,' 'specific gravity,' 'atomic weight'"—would still be employed, but "many of the beliefs presupposed by the use of these expressions would have been lost and there would appear to be an element of arbitrariness and even choice in their application which would appear very surprising to us." As a result, the possibilities for reason and proof are extremely limited: "rival and competing premises for which no further argument could be given would abound." And, tragically: "Nobody, or almost nobody, realizes that what they are doing is not natural science in any proper sense at all. For ... those contexts which would be needed to make sense of what they are doing have been lost, perhaps irretrievably."

MacIntyre suggests that moral philosophy is in just such a state of decay. It is intriguing, and somewhat disconcerting, to consider that he began his project as a criticism of the moral failings of Marxism—disconcerting, since the main attraction of Marxism over anarchism is its claim to intellectual rigor and its ability to sustain a coherent tradition over time.

Of course there are limits to this analogy of scientific revolution and post-scientific entropy. My point is not that politics are a science

In this short pamphlet, I have tried to be frank about what I see as the weaknesses of anarchist thought. However, I have also stated my own case in favor of anarchism as a political position. The two points rub together uncomfortably in my mind.

or that anarchism should be more scientific—except in the extremely broad sense that we ought to check our ideas about the world against the available evidence and revise accordingly. I merely mean to say that, between Kuhn's sketch of progress and MacIntyre's picture of intellectual disarray, today's anarchism more closely resembles the latter. What once promised to become a coherent philosophy capable of inspiring individuals, guiding a broad movement, and restructuring society, has become instead a collection of unsorted, half-remembered, often borrowed axioms and arcane cultural practices delineating a self-limiting in-group.

In this short pamphlet, I have tried to be frank about what I see as the weaknesses of anarchist thought. However, I have also stated my own case in favor of anarchism as a political position. The two points rub together uncomfortably in my mind. I confess that while I find the ideas of anarchism compelling, I recognize that my argument for them is lacking in some fundamental respects. I have thus argued as forcefully as I can manage that we must reinvigorate our tradition, beginning with a careful and demanding examination of our own premises.

Unfortunately, it is hard to picture how such a reassessment might be undertaken, and harder still to imagine that it might have the desired effect. I do not believe that a renewed theory of anarchism is likely to be born from the mind of an individual genius, nor from a distinct faction or tendency trying to push their own line, nor even from a think tank or other singular institution. All of these may of course have their place, but I expect that the interchange between them will be more important than any one participant or any single contribution. I think that the revolution in anarchist thought will emerge, if at all, from a loose association of politically engaged scholars in sustained dialogue, building on one another's theories, challenging each other's ideas, considering questions and addressing problems that sometimes overlap and sometimes dovetail.

It is not important that such scholars agree. Indeed, to productively disagree is part of their function. But *how* they disagree is important. They should wonder, consider, probe, analyze, assess—gently or forcefully, as appropriate. There are times when a budding notion needs to be fed and sheltered until it builds its own strength; and other times, when ideas will only gain definition and vitality by being challenged, tested, and even attacked. What we need is an intellectual community, joined together not by points of common doctrine, but by a shared commitment to developing and refining our thinking. It should be generally understood that our questions are as important as our answers, and that winning an argument is less desirable than learning from it.

If that is hard to imagine, it is not because the idea is vague or unrealistic; it is simply that that is almost the opposite of the political culture that we inhabit. The culture that we actually have is one characterized by norms borrowed from fundamentalism: the tendency to assume conclusions at the outset, to disregard contrary evidence, to refuse to consider competing views, to cast all those who disagree as mortal enemies, to transmute every issue into a test of virtue, to ignore all nuance and flatten all complexity and deny even the possibility of doubt. This approach is limiting in innumerable ways. It prevents us from hearing each other, from taking in new information, from challenging ourselves, from learning. We can still cast aspersions, dismissively sneer, talk past one another, or prejudge arguments without considering them. But we have lost the ability to properly disagree. Nearly every political discussion begins and ends as an exercise in cementing or policing group loyalties.

This is not a problem unique to anarchism, or even to the left. It characterizes our entire culture, from social media flame wars to White House advisors citing "alternative facts." Because these trends are so pervasive, and because their results are so dire, it becomes increasingly difficult for even small groups to preserve a space for intellectual honesty. The atmosphere is poisoned; it is difficult to breath.

This state of affairs is surely the result of numerous, disparate causes, including new technologies, the concentration of media ownership, shifts in the strategy and agendas of the two major political parties, the neoliberal restructuring of education, and postmodern skepticism (bleeding over into disregard, and then active hostility) toward the very notions of evidence, reason, and truth. To halt and reverse this vicious cycle, it is sadly not enough to produce tighter arguments or to model better practices. It is not enough to develop the ideas, we need also to develop the thinkers who are ready for the ideas. That is to say, we have to create the structures that will enable us to re-learn the necessary intellectual skills and to circulate, scrutinize, and refine our theories about the world. At certain points in history, those roles have been filled by newspapers, study groups, pamphlets, public lectures, and liberation schools, often supported by labor unions, political parties, and similar organizations. Far from being elitist distractions from bread and butter issues, such intellectual work is part of how political agency is formed, common interests discovered, and solidarity built.

For instance, as E.P. Thompson ably demonstrates in *The Making of the English Working Class*, Correspondence Societies, subversive pamphleteers, reading rooms, Mechanics' Institutes, ballad singers, and radical publishers contributed importantly to the process by which the working class came to conceive of itself, compose itself, and function *as a class*. These individuals and institutions are as important to the story he tells as are factories and looms. Thompson writes: "The making of the working class is a fact of political and cultural, as much as economic, history. . . . The changing productive relations and working conditions of the Industrial Revolution were imposed, not upon raw material, but upon the free-born Englishman—and the free-born Englishman as Paine had left him or as the Methodists had moulded him. The factory hand or stockinger was also the inheritor of Bunyan, of remembered village rights, of notions of equality before the law, of craft traditions. He was the object of massive religious indoctrination and the creator of new political traditions. The working class made itself as much as it was made."

Class-consciousness—that sense of "an identity of interests as between ... diverse groups of working people and as against the interests of other classes"—was the product of the intellectual culture as much as it was of the economic system. And the ideas emerging from and circulating within that culture animated the social movements and political organizations of the day, just as the organs of those movements fostered and fed both the traditional conceptions of liberty and the newfound radicalism, giving them space to grow, and to evolve, and to spread.

Analogous processes were undoubtedly at work in the early stages of the American civil rights movement and the women's liberation movement as well. Think about the importance of Black churches and practices such as group singing for the first, and consciousness-raising groups, locally produced but nationally circulated newsletters, and prior (often, bad) experience in the New Left for the latter. Such factors helped determine the shape, tone, and direction—the organizational forms, internal culture, and political strategy—of the emerging movements.

However, as Francesca Polletta argues in *Freedom is an Endless Meeting*, these patterns ultimately prove constraining as well. Social movements suffer crises when they outgrow their implicit models. As their established structures and practices approach their limits, movement participants are faced with an uncomfortable dilemma: either change these features to allow for further development and risk losing the distinctive character of the movement, or preserve the internal culture and organizational form at the cost of becoming increasingly insular, marginal, and stagnant.

Anarchism has faced similar crises repeatedly since it became wed to pacifism during the Second World War. That merger reshaped anarchism in a particular prefigurative and countercultural mode, organized along the lines of a friendship network and sustained by cultural practices distinguishing the scene from the surrounding society. Anarchists largely resigned themselves to their outsider status until the demise of the Soviet Union suddenly reshuffled the political deck. Then, for a while, from the peak of the anti-globalization movement until the abrupt collapse of Occupy, anarchism enjoyed

> It is probably even fair to say that the word *movement* is a misnomer: There remain individual theorists, who sometimes develop a cult-like following. There are cadre-style sects, who carefully outline a program and a line. But by and large the character of anarchism is determined by the vacillations of an ill-defined *milieu*, which adopts and discards ideas according to the mood of the moment.

a quasi-hegemonic position among American radicals. Anarchist ideas filtered through broader movements, but at the same time, they became diffuse, diluted, and indistinct.

In the early twenty-first century, some anarchists have doggedly tried to make their ideas (or sometimes, simply, themselves) relevant to each successive wave of popular unrest—anti-globalization, anti-war, Occupy, Black Lives Matter, anti-pipeline, anti-fascist, anti-Trump. Others have become increasingly wary, and sometimes hostile, toward activism, movements, and the left, even as broad concepts, and have fought to preserve a social and political distance between themselves and the progressive mainstream. Curiously, neither the evangelizing nor the sectarian impulse has served to clarify doctrinal issues. Instead, every faction and sub-faction has come to identify anarchism with their own special practices, tactics, and idioms—whether lock-downs, black blocs, consensus meetings, community gardens, or accountability processes—while retaining theories derived from other traditions (Marxist, nationalist, etc). As a result, anarchism has devolved toward competing collections of gestures signaling group membership—complex systems of means divorced from any specific ends. We identify anarchism with particular tactics, then we adopt those tactics to affirm our identity as anarchists.

Our failure, however, is not mainly intellectual, but organizational in nature: The anarchist movement has not arranged itself in such a manner that it can usefully grapple with the problems it faces—whether those be theoretical, strategic, or interpersonal. It is probably even fair to say that the word *movement* is a misnomer: There remain individual theorists, who sometimes develop a cult-like following. There are cadre-style sects, who carefully outline a program and a line. But by and large the character of anarchism is determined by the vacillations of an ill-defined *milieu*, which adopts and discards ideas according to the mood of the moment. Greek anarchists tour America, insurrectionism enjoys a vogue; Derrick Jensen reveals himself as transphobic, primitivism becomes *passé*. Communization was hot in 2010; now it's decolonization; in five more years, surely, it will be something else. Slogans, tactics, theorists, and organizational tendencies move in and out of fashion, but they follow one another almost arbitrarily, a series of abrupt shifts lacking any internal logic or sense of forward progression.

Lacking any basis for debate, disagreement becomes exceedingly dangerous. At present, the preferred means of managing it are denunciation and ostracism. To challenge, question, or even to attempt to analyze the prevailing dogma is politically suspect. This defensiveness quickly leads to an overall anti-intellectualism, though one sometimes disguised as a bullying and superior sophistication. We pose as having seen through all possible objections, so that we can avoid any careful examination of our views. Our rhetorical range shrinks to that of a spoiled adolescent: it begins at moral outrage and ends at eye-rolling disdain. A discourse conducted entirely in such a tone, and with the ideas easily expressed in such a manner, may fulfill some private emotional need for those who engage it; it will probably not, however, build a movement capable of destroying the most powerful empire in history.

Healthy movements nurture intellectual growth. They also need it. If anarchism is to thrive, either as a political force or as a body of thought, we will first need to take on the arduous task of creating the circumstances under which honesty is possible, and decency expected, and critical thinking part of the common work of the movement. We need to build toward, not simply a revolution, but at the same time, a renaissance.

If anarchism is to thrive, either as a political force or as a body of thought, we will first need to take on the arduous task of creating the circumstances under which honesty is possible, and decency expected, and critical thinking part of the common work of the movement.

Notes

The essay "Whither Anarchism?" began as a book review: Kristian Williams, "Anarchism's Mid-Century Turn," *Toward Freedom*, May 3, 2016. It also incorporates a short passage from a separate review: Kristian Williams, "Politics, Plural," *Toward Freedom*, March 5, 2015.

Thanks are owed to those who read and commented on earlier drafts of these essays, including: Zach Blue, Luis Brennan, Amelia Cates, Emily-Jane Dawson, Jamie Dawson, Peter Little, Claude Marks, Lara Messersmith-Glavin, Paul Messersmith-Glavin, Tabatha Millican, Gabriel Ryder, Josef Schneider, Spencer Sunshine, and Kevin Van Meter.

Works Cited

Murray Bookchin, *Social Anarchism or Lifestyle Anarchism: An Unbridgeable Chasm* (Edinburgh: AK Press, 1995).

Andrew Cornell, *Oppose and Propose: Lessons from Movement for a New Society* (Oakland: AK Press and the Institute for Anarchist Studies, 2011).

Andrew Cornell, *Unruly Equality: U.S. Anarchism in the Twentieth Century* (Oakland: University of California Press, 2016).

Ian Hacking, "Introductory Essay," in *The Structure of Scientific Revolutions*, fourth edition by Thomas S. Kuhn (Chicago: The University of Chicago Press, 2012).

Thomas S. Kuhn, *The Structure of Scientific Revolutions*, fourth edition (Chicago: The University of Chicago Press, 2012).

Alasdair MacIntyre, *After Virtue: A Study in Moral Theory* (Notre Dame: University of Notre Dame Press, 1984).

Francesca Polletta, *Freedom is an Endless Meeting: Democracy in American Social Movements* (Chicago: The University of Chicago Press, 2002).

Spencer Sunshine, "Post-1960 U.S. Anarchism and Social Theory [PhD. dissertation]," CUNY Graduate Center, Sociology, August 2013.

E. P. Thompson, *The Making of the English Working Class* (New York: Vintage Books, 1966).

About the author

Kristian Williams has been active in the anarchist movement since the early 1990s. He is the author, most recently, of *Between the Bullet and the Lie: Essays on Orwell* (AK Press, 2017).